The Adventures of a Canvas

Donna Kakonge is also the author of *What Happened to the Afro?*, *How to Write Creative Non-fiction*, *Spiderwoman*, *Morning English Lessons*, *In My Pocket*, editor of *Being Healthy: Selected Works from the Internet*, writer of *Do Not Know*, *My Story of Transportation*, *Draft*: *eSpirituality Chats*, reporter and producer of a CD of radio documentaries called "Nine," writer of *Journalism Stories Collection*, *Digital Journals and Numerology*, *Where I Was*, *Draft: Part Two*, *Radio and Television Announcing*, *Ugandan Travelogue* and narrated two audio stories from *Spiderwoman*; "Matoke" and "Church Sunday." The latter appeared in *Headlight*

Anthology. School Works is a collection of essays written at the undergraduate and graduate level. *Yes, School Works* are all communications essays written while she did graduate work in Montreal with Concordia University. *School Works – Other Essays* are from undergraduate work done at Carleton University in Ottawa, Canada. *The Best of Donna Magazine* highlights her online magazine which can be viewed at: http://kakonged.wordpress.com. *Old Romance* is Kakonge's 32nd book. It is a book of short stories about old romances. *How to Start Your Own Teaching and Writing Business* and *Smoking* are Kakonge's most recent books. Donna Kakonge lives in Toronto, Canada.

www.donnakakonge.com

BOOKS AND CDS BY DONNA KAKONGE

What Happened to the Afro?

How to Write Creative Non-fiction

Spiderwoman

My Roxanne

Being Healthy: Selected Works from the Internet (edited)

Do Not Know

My Story of Transportation

Draft: eSpirituality Chats

"Nine" (CD)

Journalism Stories Collection

School Works – Other Essays

Honest Psychic Chats

The Write Heart

Listening to Music

This is How the Egyptians Fell

Natural Beauty

Random Bibliography of Media Books and Internet
Resources

My Mind Book

Stories in Red and Yellow: Digging up Work Done in
Yesteryear

The Best of Donna Magazine

The Adventures of a Canvas

Donna Kakonge

Lulu.com

FIRST EDITION LULU INTERNATIONAL EDITION,

March 2010

Copyright 2010 by Donna Kay Kakonge, M.A.

All rights researched under International and Pan-American Copyright Conventions. Published in the United States by Lulu.com.

Library and Archives of Canada Cataloguing in Publication Data

Kakonge, Donna Kay Cindy
The Adventures of a Canvas
ISBN:

Book Design by Dreamstime.com

Manufactured in the United States.

The Adventures of a Signed Canvas

This is how it started…this is taken from my first mention of it in my red Moleskin journal I bought with Hyacinth Harewood at Woolfitt's:

I have this really creative idea for what to do with the piece of canvas I have left. I'm going to get people that come to the house, sign or paint their name on the canvas. Then, I will put it up in the kitchen. Wow, what a wonderful idea! You (I) can even write a book about it.

The adventures of the signed canvas. The adventure begins...

I got a call at 1:54 p.m. EST on Wednesday, December 16, 2009. I thought it was my friend John because it came up as private caller. I was in the middle of working, so I did not pick it up. Shortly afterwards, after 2:00 p.m., I called him to see if it was indeed him.

He told me that he missed me. That was kind of him. I let him know what I was up to. Finished with my marking mostly, with one more course to go, plus working on two books and this canvas painting. I did not go into detail about the canvas painting. He said he would give me a call later so we could kill some time together. That was also kind of him. I told him he would have to sign my canvas. He sounded a bit confused. If he comes over later – he would be my first signature. I'm dying to find out who will be my first signature. The wrapping is still on the canvas.

I finally got a reason to take the wrapping off the canvas. Today is Thursday, December 17, 2009 and I got my first signatures on the canvas yesterday. My Dad asked me while I was outside having a cigarette if I would like to go with my sister Lisa to pick up her daughter Oshun from pre-school. I was excited about this opportunity, especially since I had not seen my sister or my niece in quite awhile and they live not too far away.

We went down to pick up Oshun and the conversation was light. Oshun had a hot dog in her hands and Lisa offered me one because she was going back inside any way. She came back with a plain hot dog for me because I did not want any mustard or ketchup. We drove back, telling jokes and having a fun.

Once Lisa parked the car at my Dad's place, I invited her and Oshun in and Lisa signed my canvas in a purple oil pastel. Oshun wanted pink and Lisa helped her spell her name. Oshun will be turning three in March.

I ordered Pizza Pizza for them and we had a fun time while we waited, also watching Teletoon and getting adult time to watch the six o'clock news. The whole time I was with them I did not even have a cigarette. It was a fun time had by all.

Health, wealth, success, love, happiness, respect. I've had a wonderful day. I was sitting outside smoking and my neighbour Liisa came by. She said she would be back in five minutes and I looked at Mind Movies and answered some email until she rang the bell.

We sat down at my place and talked about *The Power of the Subconscious Mind.* She is going to have the Crystal Clear Maids company come in and clean for her and Kent is going to get her the book.

She signed my canvas in pink, the same colour that Oshun used.

Monday, December 21, 2009

Health, wealth, success, love, happiness, respect. I did a lot of things yesterday. I met up with Noha Hassan and we went to Faema. We had a nice time eating pizza with chicken and anchovies. We also discussed her love life and she gave me a beautiful gift of a painting with two women sitting down drinking wine. It's absolutely beautiful and looks really good in my apartment.

I also discussed numerology and feng shui with Noha. She gave me the $100 CDN she promised me, which I knew she would. She gave it to me because I am helping her edit her book. We had a good time and she met my Dad. Once we were done, she signed my canvas and we had a parting cigarette.

Saturday, December 26, 2009

I had a wonderful Christmas. I am very fortunate. I received calls from my Mom in the morning because she was unable to reach my sister. I encouraged her to just go over to my sister's house since she had already said she would be there for 12:00 p.m.

Finally, at about 1:30 p.m. I received a call from my Mom who was at my sister's house. This was the place where my family gathered for Christmas.

I went over at about 2:00 p.m. and my niece Oshun looked lovely. My mother came to the door and we all talked and had a good time. My Dad showed up shortly after I arrived.

Christmas dinner was lovely. My sister had made some Christmas cookies with my niece and all they needed was the red icing, plus the sprinkles. My niece and I sat down at her small white dining table while I added the red icing and she added the multi-coloured sprinkles. My niece Oshun favoured some of the cookies over others and added a lot of sprinkles to some and not as many to others.

My brother was on his way and my Dad left to get some rest. Christmas Day is the only day he gets off all year. He was in good spirits. Everyone was in good spirits. Once my brother arrived, I played with one of Oshun's new toys with her that her Grandma (my Mom) got her. It is a kitchen set fit for the princess that Oshun wants to be.

Oshun made me pretend water, pretend tea and pretend bread. I had a wonderful time eating with her. I was getting tired playing with her for so long that I needed to take breaks.

My Mom offered to drive me around the block to get home and out of the rain. I took up her offer because I wanted to spend time with her. My sister gave me a plate of food (my Mom had done the majority of the cooking).

My Mom came into my place and signed her name to my canvas with a red oil pastel. Now I have five signatures. The journey of the canvas continues.

My Mom has been having ailments for the past year. She finally went to a hospital on New Year's Eve Day with the encouragement of my sister Lisa.

She entered North York General Hospital at 10:30 a.m. on Thursday, December 31, 2009. She arrived back home after a battery of tests at about 7:00 p.m. I spent the time praying and reading.

It's now about 7:30 p.m. and my Mom called to let me know she was back home and my sister would be staying for the night. She joked that she was praying that she would not have to stay in the hospital either. Back home where she is originally from, St. Vincent and the Grenadines, they have a saying that if you spend New Year's Eve in a hospital, you will be there for the rest of the year. Now, she only needs to go back on Monday. Thank God for that.

Sunday, January 10, 2010

I have two more signatures on my canvas.

There is a family-owned business called Crystal Clear
Maids that I found out about from Craigslist. Sheron
James is the name of the woman who does the expert
cleaning. Kent James, her son, runs the business and does
the promotion.

About a year and a half ago, I had Hyacinth Harewood's
son Adrian tell me that I needed to have a maid clean my
home. At first I was insulted; although I knew deep down

inside that I was not doing a very good job of cleaning because I am so busy. The great thing is that Adrian offered to pay for the first cleaning because of a favour I did for him. I have been one my way to having a consistently clean home ever since.

Sheron and Kent come by about once a month or even at most once every eight weeks depending on my cash flow. Sheron does a wonderful job and she is a really good person to talk to. She's really bright and so is Kent. Their family is from Grenada and they are of South Asian origin. Recently, Sheron's aunt died in Grenada just as her aunt's daughter had papers to sponsor her in Canada. She died of cancer.

I usually have Sheron clean on Sunday mornings. During my busiest periods, it gives me a chance to do my marking on work on my book projects. She is a God-send and so is Kent.

Kent has taught me a whole bunch of things, such as how to make my own mind movies. Mind movies are visualization techniques to get what you want out of life. As well, he told me about some interesting free offers on *The Secret* website, as well as about bum marketing. Bum marketing includes marketing such as Clickbank. He's extremely business-savvy and I did an interview with him for my magazine that I am going to publish on Monday (tomorrow).

Wednesday, January 13, 2010

Dear God I pray to do the best job of my life today.

There is music playing up above. There is so much love and tranquility in this house. Dad came over twice and helped me fix my TV. He also signed my canvas. He signed it with a huge beautiful signature in black oil pastel. I'm getting there! I'm getting my canvas filled.

I read a book called *The Master Key to Success* today. It was extremely enjoyable and informative. I will write Kent James's story soon.

Everything is going well. I am having a great time and a fantastic day. Things are going great. I'm extremely blessed.

I got another signature on my canvas. On January 30, 2010, Esther Afolabi came to my house. She is an aspiring writer and a terrific storyteller. The problem is that grammatically, she does not write very well. She hired me on to do editing of her 400 plus page book and I said I would do it for $400 CDN. That is the last time I work for so little money for someone who writes as she does.

She came over and we spoke about her book, which is basically a memoir of her life. She is an extremely interesting person. She parked in my space at the front of my entrance and went to have lunch with a friend of hers who lives not too far away from where I do. She took liberties with that space and parked for way too long. By time I was ready to head out to go to a dinner party at my friend Noha's house – she was still parked there.

I worked on her manuscript and even tried to get one of my friends to do the editing and I would pay him the difference from what I was paid up front. I was paid 40 per cent up front. He had some situations to deal with and was unable to complete the work, so I continued doing it on my own.

I got to the 11th chapter and just could not take doing this tedious work anymore. The writing was so poor and the money did match all the work I was putting in. It equaled to a $1 per page. I know if I were being paid more, I would have completed the work, however last night, on Friday, February 12th, I sent the manuscript back to her and wished her luck in finding someone who would work for such a low wage.

I was also getting involved with a friend of hers named Yemi Ogunyemi who lives in Boston and he did not really help me. He ended up getting me involved with a bogus university based in Spain that is unaccredited. All in all, the situation was a learning experience and helped to understand my full worth when it comes to everything. I know now that I must only go for the top paying jobs as one of my mentors Robert Payne was kind enough to encourage me to do. Life is wonderful when you do see that everything helps you out in the end.

Monday, February 22, 2010

Today I took the canvas to be framed in a light maple type of wood at Elgin Picture and Frame close to where I live. I'm looking forward to receiving it on Wednesday. I got a renovation of my home with one wall where the couch is in yellow. I now have my South African bust of a woman in my living room. My couch is in dark brown and I have a multi-coloured leaf-designed cushion with sparkles, plus a deep orange one. I got a frame for my niece Oshun's baby picture and linen, plus three yellow towels. My place is looking beautiful. I also got brick red curtains for my living room and raspberry red ones for my office. My place is looking great. I also have a new alarm clock that is in silver with green digital numbers against a black background. Home sweet home…and my canvas that will be coming back home soon will make a beautiful addition hanging in my kitchen.

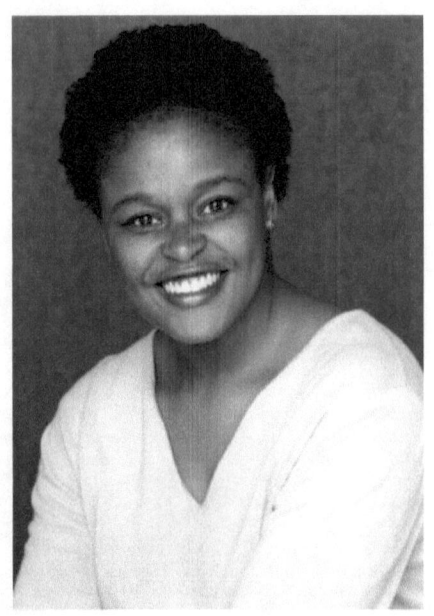

Donna Kakonge (BJ Carleton, MA Concordia) is a freelance educator, writer and broadcaster teaching journalism and communications in Toronto, Canada. She's also taught abroad. She received a Gemini nomination for work done with the Discovery Channel. Please find out more information by using the Google search engine below.

Donna's _résumé_ is also available for potential clients.

You can purchase her e-books _what Happened to the Afro?_ ,
How to Write Creative Non-fiction, and _Spiderwoman_ at her lulu.com storefront. My books are also available on Amazon's Kindle.

She's worked in every form of media, from print, radio, television and online with such places as _the Toronto Star, New Dreamhomes and Condominiums Magazine,_ the CBC, BBC, Young People's Press, One80 Youth Media Group and Vision TV. Her work and travel have taken her to such places as Belgium, Germany, Spain, Uganda and South Africa.

Check out the recent stories and audio files for exciting free information.

To contact Donna Kakonge, you can email her at: dkakonge@sympatico.ca.

Also By Donna Kakonge:

What Happened to the Afro?

This graduate research paper is a case study that sheds light on the politics of black hair.

How to Write Creative Non-fiction

Writing is one of the hardest jobs in the world, and this book will give you the help you need to crack the market. Everything you wanted to know about the writing business and how to write, with exercises included.

Spiderwoman

This book of short stories crafted over many years and originally developed in a writing workshop at Carleton University includes the experiences of a young black woman in Canada, experiencing everything from travel to family tragedy and love.

My Roxanne

Written at the age of 17 and revised later in life, this novel is the story of Roxanne and Lance – an interracial couple who go through their ups and downs.

Being Healthy: Selected Works from the Internet

This book is a compilation of works from the Internet related to health that have been edited by Donna Kakonge.

Do Not Know

This book is a collection of literary explorations of madness. A young black woman experiences the challenges and adventures of mental illness.

My Story of Transportation

This book is a memoir of Donna Kakonge's transportation experiences. Everything from roller skates to Jaguars; this is a story of how she has managed to get around.

Draft: Spirituality Chats

On a desperate search for a PhD, Donna Kakonge actually produces doctorate-level work by discovering there is more knowledge in one's common sense than meets the third eye of psychics.

Journalism Stories Collection

From newspapers and magazines such as *NuBeing International, Panache, Pride, Share* and the *Toronto Star* – Donna Kakonge creates a collection of her journalistic stories that span five years of her writing career.

The Education Generation

Perfect for professors, students and anyone in the college or university system in North America, this book has articles and columns that explore the notion of the education generation.

Digital Journals and Numerology

This book is meant to emphasize how powerful keeping a journal can be with the aid of numerology. I started writing one at the age of seven and keeping a journal has been a constant for me – more than some friends, some jobs and some family members. I used to get a thrill selecting my journals to write in. Now I have decided to try something new by using the computer that I already spend so much time on and money on to show how powerful keeping any journal...even a digital journal can be. Using the principles of numerology can also help in chronicling your life.

Other Work:

"Nine"

This is a selection of some of Donna Kakonge's radio documentaries done with the Canadian Broadcasting Corporation, as well as Radio Canada International.

"Matoke"

This audio book brings the story of Matoke from the book Spiderwoman to your ears.

"Church Sunday"

From the book Spiderwoman, an audio story of the story "Church Sunday," first published in Concordia University's *Headlight Anthology* and reviewed by the *Montreal Gazette.*

In My Pocket

This book was written to help you during the perilous times we live in.

Morning English Lessons

This is a book that is ideal for helping you hone your English skills.

Where I Was

This is a memoir of Donna Kakonge's sometimes-difficult life spent in Montreal and her move to the place she grew up in, Toronto.

Draft: Part Two

What happens when you turn to psychics for answers? You discover God.

Radio and Television Announcing

This book gives some fundamental knowledge to radio and television announcing.

Ugandan Travelogue

Donna Kakonge goes back to one of her homelands to discover where home really is.

School Works

A collection of essays Donna Kakonge has done about the black press, black journalists and ethics in filmmaking through undergraduate work at Carleton University in Ottawa, Canada and graduate work at Concordia University in Montreal, Quebec.

Yes, School Works

A collection of communication essays done at the graduate level at Concordia University in Montreal, Canada.

School Works – Other Essays

This is a collection of undergraduate arts essays done at Carleton University in Ottawa, Canada.

Honest Psychic Chats

This conversation with psychics is the last book in the series of psychic chat sessions online.

The Write Heart

This is the last in a series of books about journalism that started with How to Write Creative Non-fiction and followed with Radio and Television Announcing. This book deals with journalistic and non-fiction writing.

Story Ideas: Help For Writer's Block

This is a collection of unfinished stories that writers could pick up on to develop full-length stories.

Listening to Music

The experience of listening to Erykah Badu, Sting and India.Arie.

This is How the Egyptians Fell

Further conversations with psychics lead to a deeper understanding of how bogus this business really is. This is why the Egyptians fell.

Natural Beauty

Tips, information and advice on all forms of being a natural beauty.

Random Bibliography of Media Books and Internet Resources

This is a resource guide for media professionals, as well as students. It is also available as a free download.

My Mind Book

This is a guide of how to manifest the law of attraction.

Stories in Red and Yellow

This is a collection of fiction and non-fiction work.

www.ingramcontent.com/pod-product-compliance
Lightning Source LLC
Chambersburg PA
CBHW020948180526
45163CB00006B/2368